Created 2014
Printed in U.S.A
1ST Edition Printing 2014
Characters, Cover and Content by Author.

And you may contribute a verse
What will your verse be?

No Matter what people tell you,
Words and ideas can change the world!

FAULKNER PUBLISHING
The Legacy Continues

Vincent R Faulkner
Smyrna, Tennessee 37167

Check Out All Our Books:
EbooksByFaulkner.com
* Create Space Estore *
Amazon.com

FLASH

4

DEPLOYMENT ONE

4

PATCHES
EXPLORER
PATCHES
DISCOVERY
ADVENTURES

AIRIAL
AIRFORCE

CAMO
MARINES

SECRET
MYSTERY
MILITARY
MISSIONS

RANGER
ARMY

SECRET
MYSTERY
MILITARY
MISSIONS

GUNNER
NAVY

SECRET
MYSTERY
MILITARY
MISSIONS

SECRET
MYSTERY
MILITARY
MISSIONS

Everyone Meet FLASH 4!

FLASH 4 are very special dogs. They are PATCHES from PATCHES DISCOVERY ADVENTURES 3 brothers and 1 sister (CAMO, GUNNER, RANGER and AIRIAL) and they were all 5 born together at the same time All 5 dogs have different patches of hair that make up their coat of characters. Their character patches are what make PATCHES and FLASH 4 who they are.
Just like your character makes you who you are!

FLASH 4 has something incredible about them. Their different character patches on their hair FLASH to teach them the right thing to do every where they go! WOOF! While their sister PATCHES travels on her DISCOVERY ADVENTURES as an EXPLORER all of the FLASH 4 serve our country in the Military. RANGER is in the ARMY, CAMO is in the MARINES, GUNNER is in the NAVY and AIRIAL is in the AIRFORCE and they travel on SECRET MYSTERY MILITARY MISSIONS ARF! ARF Come and join FLASH 4 as they starts traveling on their EXCITING SECRET MYSTERY MILITARY MISSIONS

LET'S START FLASH 4'S
SECRET MYSTERY MILITARY MISSIONS

4

Meet GUNNER!

4

GUNNER is in the NAVY NSWC Naval Special Warfare Group and he is a Navy Seal on Team 1 in Search of Classified Information to Solve SECRET MYSTERY MILITARY MISSIONS

02 GUNNER'S SECRET SAFETY MYSTERY MILITARY MISSION
04 GUNNER'S SECRET TRUST MYSTERY MILITARY MISSION
06 GUNNER'S SECRET GUIDANCE MYSTERY MILITARY MISSION

" GUNNER " NAVY

GUNNER'S SECRET SAFETY MYSTERY MILITARY MISSION

GUNNER is on SAFETY patrol watching people having fun and playing on the beach in the sun

GUNNER notice's a boy is getting on a boat and not wearing a life jacket

GUNNER'S SECRET SAFETY MYSTERY MILITARY MISSION question for you is?

Should everyone practice SAFETY and wear a life jacket or not wear a life jacket when getting on to a boat or swimming?

GUNNER has a YELLOW PATCH FLASHING SAFETY!

Can you see the YELLOW PATCH FLASHING SAFETY on GUNNER?

What is the YELLOW PATCH FLASHING SAFETY on GUNNER telling you to do?

GUNNER barks: WOOF! WOOF! Always wear a life jacket when swimming or boating and practice SAFETY with everything you do!

What BIBLE VERSE teaches us about SAFETY?

SAFETY

PSALMS 4:8 I will both lay me down in peace, and sleep: for thou, LORD, only make me dwell in SAFETY.

ARF! ARF! GOD is pleased when you practice SAFETY in everything you do everyday!

03

GUNNER'S SECRET TRUST
MYSTERY MILITARY MISSION

4

GUNNER is called to a rescue a little boy who is scared to jump to safety as he is trapped in a fire on the top of a cliff

GUNNER tells the little boy to TRUST him and jump into the lifesaver below to safety.

GUNNER'S SECRET TRUST MYSTERY MILITARY MISSION question for you is?

Should the little boy TRUST GUNNER or anyone who is trying to rescue them? and jump into the life saver below to safety?

GUNNER has a YELLOW PATCH FLASHING TRUST!

Can you see the YELLOW PATCH FLASHING TRUST on GUNNER?

What is the YELLOW PATCH FLASHING TRUST on GUNNER telling you to do?

GUNNER barks: WOOF! WOOF!! Always TRUST anyone who is trying to rescue you and help you to safety like a fireman, policeman or the military.

TRUST

PROVERBS 12:22 the Lord detests lying lips, but he delights in people who are TRUSTworthy.

WOOF! GOD is pleased with people that can be TRUSTed and for

GUNNER'S SECRET GUIDANCE MYSTERY MILITARY MISSION

4

GUNNER notices a boater is headed the wrong way and in danger of crashing into the rocks!

GUNNER sends out a message on the bullhorn to offer GUIDANCE to the Boat to stop and turn around to head the right way so he will be safe.

GUNNER'S SECRET GUIDANCE MYSTERY MILITARY MISSION question for you is?

Should the boater or anyone listen to GUIDANCE from someone who is trying to help you make the right decision to be safe?

RIGHT WAY

WRONG WAY

LET'S SEE HOW GUNNER SOLVES THE
SECRET GUIDANCE MYSTERY MILITARY MISSION 4

GUNNER has a YELLOW PATCH FLASHING GUIDANCE!

Can you see the YELLOW PATCH FLASHING GUIDANCE on GUNNER?

What is the YELLOW PATCH FLASHING GUIDANCE on GUNNER telling you to do?

GUNNER barks: WOOF! WOOF!! Always listen to GUIDANCE from anyone that can help you do anything the right way like you parents, pastor or your teacher.

What BIBLE VERSE teaches us about GUIDANCE?

RIGHT WAY

WRONG WAY

GUIDANCE

PROVERBS 11:14 For lack of GUIDANCE a nation falls, but victory is won through many advisers.

GOD is pleased with those who listen to GUIDANCE that helps them do something the right way.

07

FILL IN THE MISSING WORDS IN THE BLANK SPACES CORRECTLY TO COME AND JOIN FLASH 4 ON THEIR NEXT SECRET MYSTERY MILITARY MISSIONS

PSALMS 4:8 I will both lay me down in peace, and sleep: for thou, LORD, only make me dwell in SAFETY. I will both lay me down in peace, and sleep: for thou, LORD, only make me dwell in _____.
The missing word is SAFETY.

GOD is pleased when you practice SAFETY in everything you do everyday with everyone. GOD is pleased when you practice _____ in everything you do everyday with everyone. The missing word is SAFETY.

PROVERBS 12:22 The Lord detests lying lips, but he delights in people who you can TRUST. The Lord detests lying lips, but he delights in people who you can _____. The missing word is TRUST!

WOOF! GOD is pleased with people that you can TRUST and for someone to TRUST you. GOD is pleased with people that you can _____ and for someone to _____ you. The missing word is TRUST!

PROVERBS 11:14 For lack of GUIDANCE a nation falls, but victory is won through many advisers. For lack of _____ a nation falls, but victory is won through many advisers. The missing word is GUIDANCE!

GOD is pleased with those who listen to GUIDANCE that helps them do something the right way. GOD is pleased with those who listen to _____ that helps them do something the right way. The missing word is GUIDANCE!

WOOF! GREAT JOB! YOU ARE NOW READY FOR MORE EXCITING SECRET MYSTERY MILITARY MISSIONS WITH FLASH 4 AND CAMO NEXT!

Meet CAMO!

4

CAMO is in the USMC Special Forces and is a Marine Recon Operator in Search of Top Classified Information to Solve SECRET MYSTERY MILITARY MISSIONS

" CAMO " - MARINES

CAMO'S SECRET RULES
MYSTERY MILITARY MISSION

4

CAMO is returning from a recon outing in the desert and notices a soldier is sitting under a tree.

CAMO He is not following the RULES to get in line for a drill as his commander instructed him to do.

CAMO'S SECRET RULES MYSTERY MILITARY MISSION question for you is?

Should you follow RULES that people and places you go ask you too?

LET'S SEE HOW CAMO SOLVES THE SECRET RULES MYSTERY MILITARY MISSION

4

CAMO has a YELLOW PATCH FLASHING RULES!

Can you see the YELLOW PATCH FLASHING RULES on CAMO?

What is the YELLOW PATCH FLASHING RULES on CAMO telling you to do?

CAMO barks: WOOF! WOOF!! Always listen to RULES from anyone that can help you do anything the right way like you parents, pastor or your teacher.

What BIBLE VERSE teaches us about RULES?

2 TIMOTHY 2: 5 Similarly, anyone who competes as an athlete does not receive the victor's crown except by competing according to the RULES

GOD is pleased with those who follow the RULES people or places may have to follow.

CAMO'S SECRET AFRAID MYSTERY MILITARY MISSION

4

CAMO is driving supplies to the camp and see soldiers training in the sand jumping across a water hole.

CAMO notices one soldier is AFRAID to jump across the water to the other side. His buddies are cheering him on to not be AFRAID and to give it his very best!

CAMO'S SECRET AFRAID MYSTERY MILITARY MISSION question for you is?!

Should you be AFRAID and quit or give everything your best effort you try to do?

I am AFRAID I will not

Don't be AFRAID You can make

12

LET'S SEE HOW CAMO SOLVES THE
SECRET AFRAID MYSTERY MILITARY MISSION

4

CAMO has a YELLOW PATCH FLASHING AFRAID!

Can you see the YELLOW PATCH FLASHING AFRAID on CAMO?

What is the YELLOW PATCH FLASHING AFRAID on CAMO telling you to do?

CAMO barks: WOOF! WOOF!! Do not be AFRAID. Believe in yourself that can do anything you try to do and never quit or give up.

What BIBLE VERSE teaches us about AFRAID?

Great Job! We knew you could do it

I am not AFRAID I made it across

DO NOT BE AFRAID

GENESIS 15:1 "Do not be AFRAID, Abram. I am your shield, your very great reward.

GOD is pleased with those who are not AFRAID And believe they can do anything as he has made you to be able to do.

13

CAMO'S SECRET RESCUE MYSTERY MILITARY MISSION

CAMO is leading a convoy team across the desert to their next mission location.

CAMO notices a soldier's vehicle has caught on fire and he needs someone to rescue him.

CAMO'S SECRET RESCUE MYSTERY MILITARY MISSION question for you is? ARF! ARF!

Should you RESCUE someone who is need of help or not?

Help! Please rescue me.

CAMO has a YELLOW PATCH FLASHING RESCUE!

Can you see the YELLOW PATCH FLASHING RESCUE on CAMO?

What is the YELLOW PATCH FLASHING RESCUE on CAMO telling you to do?

CAMO barks: WOOF! WOOF!! Always RESCUE, anyone who needs help as you would want someone to rescue you if you needed help.

What BIBLE VERSE teaches us about RESCUE?

JUDGES 9:17 Remember that my father fought for you and risked his life to RESCUE you from harm.

GOD is pleased with those who will RESCUE anyone that needs help to be safe.

15

FILL IN THE MISSING WORDS IN THE BLANK SPACES CORRECTLY TO COME AND JOIN FLASH 4 ON THEIR NEXT SECRET MYSTERY MILITARY MISSIONS

2 TIMOTHY 2: 5 Similarly, anyone who competes as an athlete does not receive the victor's crown except by competing according to the RULES. Similarly, anyone who competes as an athlete does not receive the victor's crown except by competing according to the _____. The missing word is RULES!

GOD is pleased with those who follow the RULES people or places may have for them to follow. GOD is pleased with those who follow the _____ people or places may have for them to follow. The missing word is RULES!

GENESIS 15:1 "Do not be AFRAID, Abram. I am your shield, your very great reward. "Do not be _____, Abram. I am your shield, your very great reward. The missing word is AFRAID!

GOD is pleased with those who are not AFRAID and believe they can do anything as he has made you to be able to do. GOD is pleased with those who are not _____ and believe they can do anything as he has made you to be able to do. The missing word is AFRAID!

JUDGES 9:17 Remember that my father fought for you and risked his life to RESCUE you from harm. Remember that my father fought for you and risked his life to _____ you from harm. The missing word is RESCUE!

GOD is pleased with those who will RESCUE anyone that needs help to be safe. GOD is pleased with those who will _____ anyone that needs help to be safe. The missing word is RESCUE!

16

WOOF! GREAT JOB! YOU ARE NOW READY FOR MORE EXCITING SECRET MYSTERY MILITARY MISSIONS WITH FLASH 4 AND AIRIAL NEXT!

Meet AIRIAL!

4

AIRIAL is in the Airforce AFSOC Special Operations Command and she is a Ace Pilot in the 1st Special Operations Wing in Search of Classified Information to Solve SECRET MYSTERY MILITARY MISSIONS

'AIRIAL' AIRFORCE

AIRIAL is flying over monitoring supply drops
to deployed soldiers.

AIRIAL sees one group of soldiers is getting a
lot more supplies than the other group is and
that is not fair. They were supposed to share equally.

AIRIAL'S SECRET BE FAIR MYSTERY MILITARY MISSION
question for you is? ARF! ARF!

LET'S SEE HOW AIRIAL SOLVES THE
SECRET BE FAIR MYSTERY MILITARY MISSION 4

AIRIAL has a YELLOW PATCH FLASHING BE FAIR!

Can you see the YELLOW PATCH FLASHING BE FAIR on AIRIAL?

What is the YELLOW PATCH FLASHING BE FAIR on AIRIAL telling you to do?

AIRIAL barks: WOOF! WOOF! Always BE FAIR. To anyone who needs help as you would want someone to rescue you if you needed help.

What BIBLE VERSE teaches us about how we should BE FAIR?

BE FAIR

LEVITICUS 19:15 Do do not show partiality to the poor or favoritism to the great, but BE FAIR as you judge your neighbor

GOD is pleased when you will BE FAIR and treat everyone equally.

19

AIRIAL'S SECRET HELP MYSTERY MILITARY MISSION

AIRIAL is flying over on a recon mission to gather intelligence.

AIRIAL sees one group of soldiers are HELPING one another to unload the supply truck and the other group of soldiers are sitting around and not HELPING the one soldier unload the supply truck

AIRIAL'S SECRET HELP MYSTERY MILITARY MISSION question for you is?

Should you be HELP someone that needs your HELP or not HELP them??

20

LET'S SEE HOW AIRIAL SOLVES THE SECRET HELP MYSTERY MILITARY MISSION

4

AIRIAL has a YELLOW PATCH FLASHING HELP!

Can you see the YELLOW PATCH FLASHING HELP on AIRIAL?

What is the YELLOW PATCH FLASHING HELP on AIRIAL telling you to do?

AIRIAL barks: WOOF! WOOF! Always HELP anyone who needs HELP as you would want someone to HELP you if you needed HELP.

What BIBLE VERSE teaches us about HELPING others?

CORINTHIANS 12:28 And God has placed in the church first of all apostles, second prophets, third teachers, then miracles, then gifts of healing, of HELPING others.

GOD is pleased with those that use his gifts to you and HELP others. 21

AIRIAL'S SECRET DIRECTIONS MYSTERY MILITARY MISSION

4

AIRIAL was sent on an emergency call to find and have an airplane change DIRECTIONS that is heading into a hurricane.

AIRIAL catches up to the airplane and radio's to change DIRECTIONS immediately to avoid danger. DANGER! DANGER! 911 CHANGE DIRECTIONS IMMEDIATELY! ARF ARF!

AIRIAL'S SECRET DIRECTIONS MYSTERY MILITARY MISSION question for you is?

Should you take DIRECTIONS from someone that is trying to help you or not take DIRECTIONS from people trying to help you?

22

AIRIAL has a YELLOW PATCH FLASHING DIRECTIONS!

Can you see the YELLOW PATCH FLASHING DIRECTIONS on AIRIAL?

What is the YELLOW PATCH FLASHING DIRECTIONS on AIRIAL telling you to do?

AIRIAL barks: WOOF! WOOF! Always follow DIRECTIONS from people that are trying to help you just as you would want anyone to listen to DIRECTIONS from you that you are trying to help.

What BIBLE VERSE teaches us about listening to DIRECTIONS from others?

DIRECTIONS

GENESIS 46:28 Now Jacob sent Judah ahead of him to Joseph to get DIRECTIONS to Goshen

GOD is pleased with those who Seek and listen to DIRECTIONS 23

FILL IN THE MISSING WORDS IN THE BLANK SPACES CORRECTLY TO COME AND JOIN FLASH 4 ON THEIR NEXT SECRET MYSTERY MILITARY MISSIONS

LEVITICUS 19:15 Do not show partiality to the poor or favoritism to the great, but BE FAIR as you judge your neighbor. Do not show partiality to the poor or favoritism to the great, but _____ as you judge your neighbor. The missing words are BE FAIR!

GOD is pleased when you treat everyone the same and BE FAIR and equal to one another. GOD is pleased when you treat everyone the same and _____ and equal to one another.
The missing words are BE FAIR!

CORINTHIANS 12:28 And God has placed in the church first of all apostles, second prophets, third teachers, then miracles, then gifts of healing, of HELPING others. CORINTHIANS 12:28 and God has placed in the church first of all apostles, second prophets, third teachers, then miracles, then gifts of healing, of _____ others.
The missing word is HELPING!

GOD is pleased with those that use his gifts to you and HELP others. GOD is pleased with those that use his gifts to you and _____ others.
The missing word is HELP!

GENESIS 46:28 Now Jacob sent Judah ahead of him to Joseph to get DIRECTIONS to Goshen. Now Jacob sent Judah ahead of him to Joseph to get _____ to Goshen. The missing word is DIRECTIONS!

GOD is pleased with those who seek, listen to and can give DIRECTIONS to help others. GOD is pleased with those who seek, listen to and can give _____ to help others. The missing word is DIRECTIONS!

WOOF! GREAT JOB! YOU ARE NOW READY FOR MORE EXCITING SECRET MYSTERY MILITARY MISSIONS WITH FLASH 4 AND RANGER NEXT!

Meet RANGER!

4

RANGER is in the Army USASOC Special Operations Command and he is a Ranger in the 1st Special Forces Operations Delta in Search of Classified Information to Solve SECRET MILITARY MYSTERY MISSIONS

"RANGER" ARMY

RANGER'S SECRET PRACTICE MYSTERY MILITARY MISSION

4

RANGER is coming back from artillery PRACTICE in the field with his tank.

RANGER sees some soldiers target training and one soldier is doing very well while the other is sitting down and not trying. The drill captain is telling the soldier he needs to PRACTICE to get better at what he is trying to do!

RANGER'S SECRET PRACTICE MILITARY MYSTERY MISSION question for you is?

RANGER has a YELLOW PATCH FLASHING PRACTICE!

Can you see the YELLOW PATCH FLASHING PRACTICE on RANGER?

What is the YELLOW PATCH FLASHING PRACTICE on RANGER telling you to do?

RANGER barks: WOOF! WOOF! Always PRACTICE what you are trying to do! PRACTICE makes you be the best you that you can be!

What BIBLE VERSE teaches us that we should PRACTICE what we do?

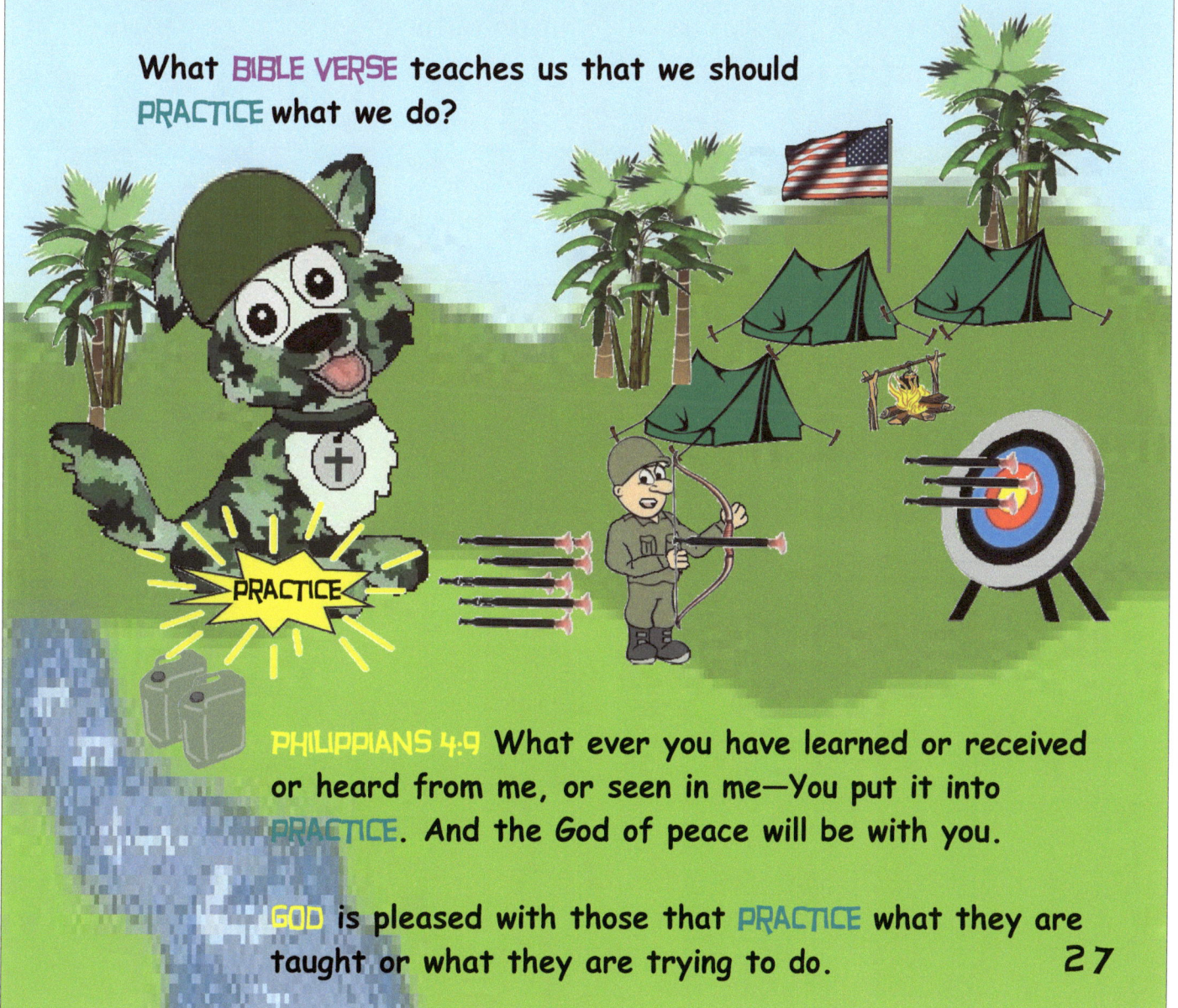

PRACTICE

PHILIPPIANS 4:9 What ever you have learned or received or heard from me, or seen in me—You put it into PRACTICE. And the God of peace will be with you.

GOD is pleased with those that PRACTICE what they are taught or what they are trying to do.

RANGER'S SECRET WORK
MYSTERY MILITARY MISSION

4

RANGER is driving the water supply truck and waiting for it to be loaded to take water to thirsty villagers all over the jungle.

RANGER sees some soldiers sitting and not WORKING like the other soldiers WORKING to load the water supply truck for the thirsty villagers!

RANGER'S SECRET WORK MILITARY MYSTERY MISSION question for you is?

Should you WORK or not WORK and do nothing with other people WORKING or by yourself?

28

LET'S SEE HOW RANGER SOLVES THE
SECRET WORK MYSTERY MILITARY MISSION 4

RANGER has a YELLOW PATCH FLASHING WORK!!

Can you see the YELLOW PATCH FLASHING WORK on RANGER?

What is the YELLOW PATCH FLASHING WORK on RANGER telling you to do?

RANGER barks: WOOF! WOOF! Always WORK by yourself and with others who are WORKING doing things like chores, homework, helping others or your job!

PROVERBS 12:14 From the fruit of their lips people are filled with good things, and the WORK of their hands brings them reward.

GOD is so pleased with those that WORK at what they do and do not quit or give up as he blesses them.

29

RANGER is washing his army hummer vehicle to keep it CLEAN and take care of it so it can be the best it can be when RANGER drives it on missions.

RANGER sees another soldier who is not CLEAN and is very dirty and muddy with his army hummer vehicle but the soldier said he does not want to CLEAN himself or the army hummer vehicle to take care of it

RANGER'S SECRET CLEAN MYSTERY MILITARY MISSION question for you is?

Should you keep yourself CLEAN and your clothes, your bedroom, your bicycle and your families vehicle that you ride in or drive or should you be dirty?

RANGER has a YELLOW PATCH FLASHING CLEAN!

Can you see the YELLOW PATCH FLASHING CLEAN on RANGER?

What is the YELLOW PATCH FLASHING CLEAN on RANGER telling you to do?

RANGER barks: WOOF! WOOF! Always make sure you are CLEAN and everything like your clothes, bedroom, and even the vehicle you drive are CLEAN too!

What BIBLE VERSE teaches us about being CLEAN?

CLEAN

LEVITICUS 10:10 So that you can distinguish between the holy and the common, between the unclean and the CLEAN

GOD is pleased with those that keep them selves CLEAN as being CLEAN is being Holy.

FILL IN THE MISSING WORDS IN THE BLANK SPACES CORRECTLY TO COME AND JOIN FLASH 4 ON THEIR NEXT SECRET MYSTERY MILITARY MISSIONS IN DEPLOYMENT TWO

PHILIPPIANS 4:9 Whatever you have learned or received or heard from me, or seen in me—You put it into PRACTICE. and the God of peace will be with you. Whatever you have learned or received or heard from me, or seen in me—You put it into _____. and the God of peace will be with you. The missing word is PRACTICE!

GOD is pleased with those that PRACTICE the what they are taught or trying to do with everything they do. GOD is pleased with those that _____ the what they are taught or trying to do with everything they do. The missing word is PRACTICE!

PROVERBS 12:14 From the fruit of their lips people are filled with good things, and the WORK of their hands brings them reward. From the fruit of their lips people are filled with good things, and the _____ of their hands brings them reward. The missing word is WORK!

GOD is so pleased with those that WORK at what they do and do not quit or give up he blesses them. GOD is so pleased with those that _____ at what they do and do not quit or give up he blesses them. The missing word is WORK!

LEVITICUS 10:10 So that you can distinguish between the holy and the common, between the unclean and the CLEAN. LEVITICUS 10:10 So that you can distinguish between the holy and the common, between the unclean and the _____. The missing word is CLEAN!

GOD is pleased with those that keep them selves CLEAN as being CLEAN is being Holy. GOD is pleased with those that keep them selves _____ as being _____ is being Holy. The missing words are CLEAN!

WOOF! GREAT JOB! YOU ARE NOW READY FOR MORE EXCITING SECRET MYSTERY MILITARY MISSIONS WITH FLASH 4 IN DEPLOYMENT TWO!